What Others Are Saying About

Family Worship for the Christmas Season

"In a day when having regular family worship is no longer a foregone conclusion (even among conservative Evangelicals), Ray Rhodes provides a wonderful impetus to start: a month of clear, biblical, practical devotions celebrating the birth of King Jesus. Hopefully, those who begin this Christmas using this excellent resource will continue gathering daily at the family altar throughout the coming year." David W. Bailey, Ph.D., Author, *Speaking the Truth in Love: The Life and Legacy of Roger Nicole*

"Ray Rhodes has written a wonderfully creative book on family worship for the Christmas season. For a father or mother to take their children through these precious truths would create a fond memory that the children would have for the rest of their life. The book is doctrinally sound, well written, and greatly honoring to our Lord. I'm going to order three copies right now!" Martha Peace, Biblical Counselor and author of *The Excellent Wife*

"The Christmas season is a great time for daily family worship. If you've never enjoyed family worship on a consistent basis, there's no better time to start. Whether your family already enjoys the biblical and historic Christian practice of family worship or you're just beginning, consider using Ray Rhodes' engaging *Family Worship for the Christmas Season* this December." - Dr. Donald S. Whitney, author of *Spiritual Disciplines of the Christian Life* and *Family Worship: In the Bible, in History, and in Your Home.*

FAMILY WORSHIP
FOR THE CHRISTMAS SEASON

FAMILY WORSHIP

FOR

THE CHRISTMAS SEASON

Ray Rhodes, Jr.

Solid Ground Christian Books
Birmingham, Alabama USA

Solid Ground Christian Books
PO Box 660132
Vestavia Hills AL 35266
205-443-0311
sgcb@charter.net
www.solid-ground-books.com

FAMILY WORSHIP FOR THE CHRISTMAS SEASON

Ray Rhodes, Jr.

First edition printed in October 2007

Cover design by Borgo Design, Tuscaloosa, AL
Contact them at **borgogirl@bellsouth.net**

Scripture references in this book are from the New King James Version of the Bible.

ISBN: 1-59925-1299

This Christmas book is dedicated to my wife Lori and our five daughters: Rachel, Hannah, Sarah, Mary and Lydia. Lori and I are celebrating our twentieth Christmas together as husband and wife. The Lord has blessed us with five priceless presents over these twenty years. They all came wrapped in pink.

Special Thanks

To my wife Lori who gave many hours of her time reading and helping with this book. On her last reading she said, "It's even better than I remembered." Those are the words of a sweet wife.

To Rachel, Hannah, Sarah, Mary and Lydia—Thank you for your help and encouragement. I love being your daddy and look forward to decorating the tree.

To my parents who still today help to make Christmas very special. From Crawfordville to Robinson we have enjoyed some great Christmas seasons! The Christmas candy is always anticipated and is never a disappointment.

To my grandmother (Nanny, age 93) and my Aunt Thelma who are still fresh reminders of years of Christmas traditions.

To my sisters and their families who have helped stir up the laughter over the years.

To my brother Andrew and his family—I waited a long time for you Andrew—thanks for showing up.

To my mother-in-law who delivered to me my most precious gift. Thank you for your generosity to our family at Christmas and always.

To my father-in-law who takes time for my girls. They are glad to call you Papa.

To my longtime friend David and his family who are such a blessing to my family and me. Thanks David for your help in editing this book.

To my fellow pastor Kevin and his family whom the Lord sent to us at just the right time.

To Grace Community Church of North Georgia—a great source of strength to our family.

Any similarities in this book to any other book are not intentional. This book was produced from Bible study, years of Christmas traditions and favorite family memories.

"Telling to the generation to come the praises of the LORD and His strength and His wonderful works that He has done." (Psalm 78:4)

Table of Contents

A Perspective from Lori Rhodes

When Ray and I got married I knew he was a godly man who wanted to serve the Lord in full time ministry. Little did I know that he was also a king—actually, *the* king of traditions. Early in our marriage we began traditions such as eating pizza in front of the television, having company at New Year's, and cutting our own Christmas tree with Ray always wearing a red flannel shirt no matter what the weather. I was not used to such traditions so this was wonderful to me.

One of the traditions I treasure most is the reading of Luke chapter 2. When Ray was growing up, his father would read the Christmas story to all the children just before they went to bed on Christmas Eve. On our first Christmas together we spent the night in his parents' home. When they all pulled out Bibles and gathered to read, I was very impressed. Here was a dad who really wanted his children to know the true meaning of Christmas.

Gradually, as our family grew, so did our traditions. We have customs for almost every month that "must" be done. During the fall and holiday seasons there are trips to Old Salem, the pumpkin farm and the apple house that just can't be missed. When the days turn cooler and we get our Christmas tree, tradition reigns.

We believe that God-centered traditions can point our children to God. Reading the Christmas story is one of those that has helped shape our family. Our daughter Mary was born in early January and her name came from family Bible readings during December. I can't remember a season in which we didn't gather the little ones onto our laps, light candles, and sing *Silent Night*. Memories of night rides to look at lights are treasured.

Reading Scripture is not just a tradition; it's a way of life. Our family revolves around our family Bible times. As we gather every night to read the Bible, the children are comforted by the Word and the continuance of the gathering. We are seeking to be faithful to our Lord and to His people throughout history who passed down the truth of a great God.

Perhaps family worship times have not characterized your home. Why not start today? And throughout the day look for opportunities to share with your children and others of the goodness of God. You will likely discover that children can learn a lot about God while rolling their hands in dough that will be used to make cookies. They will also learn how to bless their neighbor by taking those cookies next door and sharing them.

Family life is a great blessing from God. What a privilege God has given by teaching us to worship God as a family. We plan to go through this book day by day in December. Will you join us and share these wonderful activities with your family?

Lori Rhodes

Opening Statement

Having a house filled with daughters keeps my mind busy. My thoughts include the fact that the seatbelt needs to be replaced on seat number eight in our van. The belt needs replacing because one of my daughters decided to tie the belt in a knot just before she released the belt back into its slot. A number of great minds have attempted to unravel the knot, but to no avail.

Living in a home with 6 young women (my wife included) is quite an adventure. Of course there is the challenge of attempting to "borrow" MY bathroom. Yet there is also the quest of seeking to get into the hearts and minds of my girls. Sometimes it seems like trying to unravel the knot in our seatbelt—impossible. However, the Lord in His grace allows me glimpses into the hearts of my wife and daughters. I am richer for each glimpse. The six girls that surround my life with beauty present a great opportunity for me and for us as a family. We have an opportunity and vision to glorify God!

Family life is important, but not as an end in itself. The objective is not simply a happy family; God Himself is the goal. When God, instead of family, is the objective then the garden in which the family is planted can grow and produce sweet fruit (Psalm 128)!

This guide is designed to encourage family worship. God can be worshipped in a general way as, for example, the sunrise and the sunset are seized to draw attention to the greatness of God in creation. Creation is a God-glorifying classroom. This classroom should be used to instruct our children concerning the creative genius of our great God. More specifically, God can be worshipped in our families during biblically-driven family gatherings. In these gatherings the Scripture is read, God is sought in prayer and songs of praise are sung. Family worship is seeking to impress upon each member of the family the character of God so that they might know who God is and respond joyfully to the truth about Him! Ultimately, of course, no one has the power to imprint God upon the hearts of others. We are dependent on God. He has chosen to use His Word through His people to lead others to know Him. Therefore, we have every reason to be hopeful in our efforts to teach our children (and others) when we are faithful to use the means that God has promised to bless. In the pages that follow you will find assistance in applying God's Word in your daily family gatherings.

It is God's design that we see the family in a larger, more visionary context. My children are the children of previous generations (Psalm 78:4) and they are arrows of God's glory to be launched into future generations (Psalm 78:6; 127:3-5). Godly family life requires us to look backwards to those who have gone before and to look forward to those who will come after us. We are to learn the lessons of God's providence in the past and send those lessons into the future. This sort of vision encourages hope, faithfulness and worship in a family. I pray that your family will have a vision for God's glory this Christmas season! *Merry Christmas!*

Introduction

This book is designed to help you and your family to focus on Christ during the Christmas season. Family worship is most effective as you creatively find ways to involve everyone in your home. Make sure that each member of your family (even the very young ones) has his own copy of the Bible so that they may grow in their appreciation for truth. Feel free to adapt the daily lessons and activities to your family. Consider adding hymn singing to every day's activities. It has often been suggested that, generally speaking, family worship should include: Scripture reading, singing, and prayer. In our family we often include some reading from a good book like *The Pilgrim's Progress*. We generally have a brief time of Bible reading each morning and a more extended time of family worship in the evening.

On the one hand, the thought of leading family worship should be humbling. On the other hand, if you are a Christian, then the Holy Spirit lives within you and will enable you in your faithful pursuits. The thought of leading family worship should not be inappropriately intimidating. You are not preaching a lengthy sermon; rather, you are simply seeking to expose your family to the truth. You should encourage each member of your family to be reading the Bible on their own. I often challenge my wife and children to read from the Bible before they read anything else each morning. Family worship is exciting. You are taking ancient truth, investing it in the life of your family and aiming for the future worship of God (Psalm 78:1-8). So get started, and enjoy drawing near unto God with your family.

Note: Even if you do not presently have children living with you, the worship of God in your home should still be a part of your life. If you are married with no children at home, single, or widowed then this guide can be adapted to help you get started on a daily journey of learning more about God.

As you read through this resource for family worship you will find a variety of helps including a catechism and extra worship activities for each Lord's Day in the month.

December 1st

Scripture Reading

Psalm 78:1-8

Christians are not isolated from either the past or the future. You stand upon the shoulders of the faithful who have gone before you even as you invest in those who will follow you. During this month of Christmas devotions look for ways to teach your children about their rich heritage of faith. Read from the Bible. Show them pictures of great Christian leaders in history. Tell your children about their grandparents and great-grandparents!

Lead your family in a reading of the opening sentences of *The Apostle's Creed* which was developed by Christians in the early centuries of the church. Your goal today is to give your children a rich sense of history.

I believe in God, the Father Almighty,
Maker of heaven and earth.
And in Jesus Christ his only Son, our Lord;
who was conceived by the Holy Ghost, born of
the Virgin Mary...

Read with and remind your family:
1. God is the Creator (Genesis 1:1).
2. Jesus is His only Son (John 3:16).
3. Jesus is the Lord (Philippians 2:5-11).
4. Jesus is truly human, born of the Virgin Mary (Luke 1:26-28; 2:7).

Prayer

Our Father in heaven we acknowledge that You are Almighty God the Creator of all things. We praise You that You have sent Your one and only Son to be our Lord. We acknowledge that He is fully God and fully man, born of the Virgin Mary. Help us as a family to focus on Jesus this Christmas season and always. Amen.

December 2nd

Scripture Reading

Luke 1:46-55

As a child, I remember thinking that the
Christmas season really began with the
singing of the first Christmas hymn at
church. Though the trappings of Christmas
were all around, I still associated the
celebration of Christmas with the people of
God. The Bible contains what we may call
the "First Christmas Carol." It was not
sung by angels but by the Virgin Mary
(Luke 1:46-55).

Family Activity

Give each family member a sheet of paper
and a pencil, pen or crayon. Have
everyone list aspects of God's character

found in Mary's Christmas song. Compare results and make a master list to place on your refrigerator. Use the list to help you call to mind the grace, might, holiness, and mercy of God. Sing a favorite Christmas carol or write a new one! It would be a great idea (if you don't already own one) to purchase a copy of a good biblically-based hymnal to use in family devotion times.

Prayer

Our Father in heaven we praise You that You are God the Savior and that You have regarded lowly sinners like us. Help us to rejoice in You. We acknowledge Your might, holiness, mercy, strength, sovereignty and goodness. Amen.

December 3rd

Scripture Reading

Luke 2:25-35

Glory is an expressive word that is used in a variety of contexts. One might speak of the *glory* of winning a sport's championship. Even a meal might be called *glorious*. However, the word glory is best reserved for the things of God and especially for the Son of God. The Hebrew word for glory is *kabod* which derives from a verb meaning to "be heavy." When we speak of God's glory we are saying that He is weighty, that His essence is ultimately substantive. Simeon said of the baby that he held in his arms, "A light to bring revelation to the Gentiles, and the glory of Your people Israel" (Luke 2:32). The angels proclaimed, "Glory to God in the highest and on earth peace, goodwill toward men!" Jesus was truly glorious. To speak of the glory of Christ is to draw attention to His magnificence, brilliance, brightness, authority and sheer weightiness.

Family Activity

Take a Bible concordance and look up passages that contain the word glory. With your children write down several references and look for ways in which the word is used. Write the word glory across the top of a large sheet of paper and put words beneath each letter that give insight into the meaning of the word. For example you might put the word "great" beneath the G.

Prayer

Almighty God, You alone are glorious beyond compare. Your brilliance is evident in the world that You created and through the Scriptures that You inspired. Help us, O Lord, to take You seriously. You are a weighty God. Amen.

December 4th

Scripture Reading

Revelation 19:11-16

Jesus is coming soon! One often hears such a statement in reference to the Second Coming of Christ. In reality no one knows how soon it will be before Jesus returns to the earth. We should, however, always live in anticipation of His return. Think of what it must have been like for Joseph and Mary when they heard the news from an angel that Jesus would be arriving soon. Read Matthew 1:18-25 and Luke 1:26-38. Truly Joseph and Mary could say that Jesus is coming soon.

Family Activity

Put together a paper chain and place it near the breakfast table. Create a link for each remaining day through Christmas day. Each morning at breakfast break a link and watch the chain shorten. Help your children to anticipate Christmas morning and imagine what Joseph and Mary must have been thinking as their first Christmas drew near.

Prayer

Our Father in heaven, thank You for sending Your Son. Thank You for choosing Joseph and Mary. Help us as we prepare our home for Christmas to live our lives anticipating Your Second Coming. Amen.

December 5th

Scripture Reading

Matthew 1:1-17

What are some of your treasured family traditions? Very soon after Thanksgiving Day we journey to a Christmas tree farm in Ellijay, Georgia. We choose and cut our tree and then take it home to decorate. This is an exciting time for our family. Traditions help to keep a family connected with former generations. Some of the things that we do with our children during the holidays are directly related to things that we did as children, and our parents did before us. Spend some time talking about family traditions with your children. As you ponder the Scripture reading for today, help your children to understand the importance of the genealogy of Christ.

Each family listed probably had a variety of both biblically-ordained and other family traditions. A tradition is a valued family activity which has been a part of one's life over an extended period of time. A tradition can be a tool of learning that illustrates the goodness of God. Therefore, our traditions should bring God glory and be helpful in the strengthening of family life.

Family Activity

Purchase a blank book and write of traditions from your childhood that are now a part of your immediate family. Write down new and valued family activities. Your handwritten book will become a treasure for future generations. Luke 1: 46-47 records the words of Mary when she said "My soul magnifies the Lord, and my spirit has rejoiced in God my Savior." Rejoice that Jesus is the Lord and that He has blessed you with family, friends and traditions. Reminisce about family members from as many generations as you can recall.

Prayer

Thank You God for connecting us to the past and the future. Our traditions are one way that we are reminded of our larger family. Help us in our traditions to magnify the Lord. Amen.

December 6th

Scripture Reading

Isaiah 9:6-7

It is a neat thing to receive a birth announcement. Often times the announcement comes with a picture of the newborn baby that has arrived. Though we know in advance when a friend or family member is expecting a baby, the official birth announcement does not arrive until the baby is born. The Bible, however, announced the birth of Jesus many years before He was born. Passages like Isaiah 7:14, 9:6-7 and Micah 5:2 are promises of One who was to come in the future. You might say that the birth announcement of Jesus was sent hundreds of years before He actually arrived on the earth. The faithful Hebrew people looked forward to His coming.

Family Activity

Ask your children how they feel about a promise that is made to them. Talk to them about the importance of keeping a promise. People sometimes break their promises but God never does. Create a family Christmas announcement. It could read something like this... "On December 25th the Jones family will (God-willing) celebrate the birth of Jesus Christ by sharing gifts and a meal." Copy Bible promises about the coming of Jesus onto the announcement and hang it in a prominent place or mail it to a friend. Now you have a paper chain and a Christmas announcement to help build anticipation for Christmas day.

Prayer

Our Father in heaven, thank You for keeping Your Word. Thank You for the promise of Jesus. Please help our family to honor You when we make promises. Amen.

December 7th

Scripture Reading

Matthew 28:18-20

Christmas is about much more than your family and is much larger than your living room. The vision of Christmas stretches from before time and beyond time. The Bible speaks of the "...hope of eternal life which God, who cannot lie, promised before time began" (Titus 1:2). The birth of Jesus was planned before the world was ever created. God's plan of redemption was orchestrated "before time began." The Bible also teaches that the salvation of God's people by Christ will bring Him glory in the ages to come "that in the ages to come He might show the exceeding riches of His grace in His kindness toward us in Christ Jesus" (Ephesians 2:7). When God sent His Son into the world it was the outworking of His plan that began before time and continues into eternity. John 3:16 reminds us of God's amazing love for the world demonstrated in the sending of Jesus. This is what we are embracing afresh at Christmas. Our vision of Christmas must look back to eternity past, forward to eternity future and embrace a large vision for missions to the entire world. That is what motivated Paul to say, "Therefore I endure all things for the sake of the elect, that they also may obtain the salvation which is in Christ Jesus with eternal glory" (2 Timothy 2:10).

Family Activity

Do a "Google" search for Christmas customs around the world. Write down some of the more interesting Christmas traditions of people from a variety of cultural backgrounds. Mark the places on a world map and pray that the people of that region would hear and believe the gospel of Jesus Christ. Have your pastor help you to discover missionaries who are serving in those areas. Pray for them by name and consider writing a letter of encouragement to them. Put a collection box near your Christmas tree that will be used to collect coins for missions giving. The Scripture reading for today is a reminder that we are to take the gospel to the entire world.

Prayer

Our Father in Heaven, we pray that Your character would be recognized as great throughout the world. Please encourage and enable Your missionaries to be faithful. Please help our family and church to be faithful to share Christ during the Christmas season and always. Amen.

December 8th

Scripture Reading

John 1:1-14

Both the book of Genesis and the book of John open with the same phrase, "In the beginning..." God, who had no beginning, created the beginning. Our Scripture passage today teaches the two natures of Christ. The two natures of Christ can be difficult to understand. The Son of God is eternal (John 1:1) and the Son of God became man (John 1:14). Jesus is the God/Man. He is fully God and fully man. This is a big truth that has been the source of much discussion since the birth of Jesus. It was in becoming man that Jesus humbled Himself, died on the cross and was raised from the dead. Jesus lived on this earth and never sinned. That is important because had Jesus sinned, we would not have a Savior. It is because Jesus never sinned that we can, by faith, be made right with God (2 Corinthians 5:21). "In the beginning" we find the Word (Jesus) already existing face-to-face with the Father. He is God. And yet Jesus "became flesh and dwelt among us" (John 1:14).

Family Activity

The truth of the two natures of Christ inspires worship. Have each member of your family bow their heads and meditate on the awesomeness of the God/Man. Let silence fill the room and after a few minutes lead your family in giving thanks to our great God.

Prayer

Our Lord we acknowledge the mysteries of Christmas that we cannot fully comprehend. Strengthen our faith that we might believe and love the truth that Your Word teaches about Your Son. Amen.

December 9th

Scripture Reading

Hebrews 10:24-25

The church is a "one another community of love." It is with the people of God that we find (and give) encouragement. Often during the Christmas season people are sad for a variety of reasons. Being with God's people helps us look to Jesus for joy in the midst of difficulty. It is easy during this time of year to lose focus and to become materialistic. Participating in the committed life of a faithful church will help you stay focused on Christ. How can you encourage love and good works among the people of God?

Family Activity

If your church has a weekly church bulletin then seek to get your copy in advance. Use the bulletin to help you prepare for the next Lord's Day gathering with the people of God. Walk through the order of service with your family. Pray for your pastor and other church leaders. Sing a verse of each hymn that will be a part of the Lord's Day service.

Prayer

Our Father in heaven, we pray that You will be truly worshipped by Your people each time we gather. Please help our family to appreciate the family of God. Help us to be sensitive to how we can encourage love and good deeds among our fellow Christians. Help us to be aware of those that may be especially sad during this Christmas season. Amen.

December 10th

Scripture Reading

Micah 5:1-2

"*O Little Town of Bethlehem*" is one of the all-time favorite Christmas hymns. The title and the lyrics draw attention to the adjective "little." That word is taken directly from our Scripture reading for today. *But you, Bethlehem Ephrathah, though you are little among the thousands of Judah, yet out of you shall come forth to Me the One to be ruler in Israel, whose goings forth are from of old, from everlasting" (Micah 5:2).* Folks throughout history have associated greatness with that which is large. Think of a common question that is often asked about a particular local church; "How many folks do you have there?" Or perhaps the interest is on the size of the building or the acreage of the property. People, buildings and property are not bad things, but they may not reveal the true greatness of a church. The same is true with the word little. There is nothing necessarily virtuous about being little, but don't underestimate what God may do through that which appears to be small in size or influence. God is most magnified when we recognize how little we are in comparison to His greatness. We can be confident that regardless of how "little" we are, if we know and love God He will use us for His glory.

Family Activity

Make sure everyone in your family has a Bible. Read Mark 6:32-44; 8:1-10; 2 Corinthians 4:7. Divide the passages up between each member of your family. Each text draws attention to the greatness of God and how He takes that which is small and by His power does a great work. What are some "little" things that you can point to that have been used by God for a big purpose? Ask everyone in your family to respond.

Prayer

Our Father in heaven, we thank You for making Yourself known through Jesus Christ Your Son. We worship Jesus because Your greatness is evident in how You take small things and use them in such a way that You are glorified. Amen.

December 11th

Scripture Reading

Luke 2:30-32

Lights are a vital part of our Christmas celebrations. The Christmas tree is filled with lights. We light candles on an Advent Wreath and even have candlelight services at our church. Many people drape their homes in lights. Simeon referred to Jesus as "a light" in Luke 2:32. Jesus referred to His disciples as "light" in Matthew 5:14. As the Christian shines as a light, his godly life points to the brightness of Jesus.

Family Activity

Load the family in your vehicle and take a night drive through town. Survey the many different kinds of lights and decorations that you notice. You will likely see many thousands of lights on even a short drive around town. Sing holiday songs together in the car and enjoy the beauty of the sparkling lights against the night sky. Stop by a local restaurant and enjoy some dessert. Talk about the significance of Jesus as the Light. He is our clarity in a world of confusion and darkness. Think of ways that your family can shine as lights in a world that is shrouded by sin.

Prayer

Our Father in heaven, thank You that Jesus has come and brought light into a world darkened in sin. Thank You for the hope that we have in Christ. Help our family to shine as bright lights in a world of darkness. May our lives point to Jesus who is the light of the world. Amen.

December 12th

Scripture Reading

Romans 6:23 and Romans 3:9-23

Romans 6:23 reminds us that sin has a price and that price is death. Why raise the issues of sin and death during a season in which the atmosphere is aglow with singing "Joy to the World?"

If we do not understand something of our sin, then we cannot appreciate the coming of Jesus to the manger in Bethlehem, nor can we grasp the significance of His death on the Cross. The Bible says that "Christ Jesus has come into the world to save sinners" (I Timothy 1:15). We are sinners. Left in our sin we have only death to expect with no hope of life everlasting with God. Our sin must be taken away in order for us to have the hope of one day seeing God and for us to be able to live for His glory now. Jesus came to save sinners. To receive the benefits of His birth, life, death and resurrection, it is essential that we repent of our sins and trust in Christ.

Family Activity

Look up or draw a picture of a rustic cradle and cross. Ask the question: Why did Jesus come to the earth? Give the answer: "To save sinners." Ask, "How do you know?" Answer, "The Bible says that Christ Jesus came into the world to save sinners." Christmas is about Jesus coming to deal with the sin of His people!

Prayer

Our Father in heaven, thank You for Your amazing love in sending Jesus to be born and to die. Help us to see how awful sin is and how amazing Your grace is. Amen.

December 13

Scripture Reading

I Thessalonians 1:1-10

Since Jesus came to save sinners what then is to be our response to such grace? The answer is found in the word repent. Repentance refers to a change of direction. When a person, through the lens of Scripture and by God's grace, sees himself as a sinner in need of a Savior and turns in faith to Christ for salvation, we call that repentance. Paul said of the Thessalonian Christians that they had "turned to God from idols to serve the living and true God" (I Thessalonians 1:9). You must repent of your sins in order to be saved. Even if you are a Christian, your life should be characterized by repentance (Revelation 2:5; 2 Corinthians 7:1-12).

Family Activity

When a person is going away from Christ they are going the wrong way. Find a way to illustrate with your children that our sin puts us on a highway going the wrong direction. If we remain on the highway we can be certain that great danger awaits us. Show them a picture of a "wrong way" sign and then a "U-Turn" sign. Remind them that if they will U-Turn from their sins and turn in faith to Christ, then they will be saved from their sins.

Prayer

Our Father in heaven, thank You for the gift of repentance. Help our family to take sin seriously by turning away from sin and to You. Amen.

December 14th

Scripture Reading

Psalm 19

God has revealed Himself to us! That is good news. *How* has God made Himself known to us? We often speak of the "4 C's of Revelation" to our children.

Creation: God has made Himself known by all that He has made (Psalm 19:1; Romans 1:20). Creation declares the power, creativity and greatness of God.

Conscience: Conscience is the voice-box inside a person that commends him when he does right and convicts him when he does wrong (Romans 2:15). God has written on the conscience of man the fact that there is right and wrong and there is One to whom we must give account.

Common Grace: Of course God's grace is anything but common. But common grace refers to grace that is common to mankind in general. Rain, sunshine and fruitful seasons are all a witness to the fact that there is a God and He is good (Acts 14:17).

Canon: By canon we are referring to the sixty-six books that make up the Bible. Creation, conscience, and common grace tell us many great things about God and we are accountable for such knowledge. However the first three "C's" do not tell us what we need to know in order to be forgiven of our sins and to be made right with God. We are dependent on the canon of Scripture for that information (2 Timothy 3:15). Creation, conscience, and common grace are sufficient to tell us what they are designed to tell about God, but they are not sufficient to lead us to a saving knowledge of Jesus Christ. We need the Bible. In the Bible we learn that God has made Himself savingly known through Christ.

Family Activity

Think of ways to teach your family the "4 C's" of revelation. Take a trip outdoors with a journal and write down three amazing things that you see that give evidence that God is the creator. Talk with your children about right and wrong. Ask them how they feel when they do wrong. Speak to them about the importance of having a sensitive conscience. Remember to consider the rain, sunshine and your meals and to thank God for His common grace. Read from "The Christmas Story" in the Bible (Luke 1-2; Matthew 1) and thank God for the canon of Scripture.

Prayer

Our Father, thank You for making Yourself known to us. We could not know anything about You if You had not chosen to write Your character on creation, conscience and common grace. We thank You for those things but especially for the canon of Scripture. Amen.

December 15th

Scripture Reading

Luke 1:11-13, 26-30; 2:9-14.

The verses above are some of the "Christmas" verses that refer to angels. The word angel simply means "messenger." There is in our culture an interest in angels. Go to a local gift shop and you will notice a variety of perspectives on angels. Pictures, statues and ornaments of angels often portray these mysterious beings as soft and feminine, or as cute little overweight babies with wings. The Bible never portrays angels in infant or feminine form. Angels are strong, masculine-like beings whose presence often strikes fear into the hearts of those who see or hear from them. Therefore, in the Bible, we find angels uttering the words "Do not be afraid" or "Fear not." As awesome as angels are, they are never to be worshipped. In fact, an angel reminded the apostle John that God alone is to be worshipped (Revelation 19:10).

Family Activity

The movie, "It's A Wonderful Life" is watched by many families each year during the Christmas season. Jimmy Stewart stars in this warm, funny and thought-provoking movie. The movie also features a clumsy but lovable angel named Clarence. Consider renting this movie and watch half of it tonight and the other half tomorrow night. Have each member of your family jot down key themes from the movie. Especially note the characteristics of Clarence. Tomorrow take the opportunity to contrast Clarence the angel with the angels that you find in Scripture.

Prayer

Our Father in heaven, thank You for painting the Christmas story with such awesome pictures. The angels are another reminder of your greatness. Help us to have a correct understanding of angels and to guard against the faulty views presented in our culture. Help us to worship You. Amen.

December 16th

Scripture Reading

Isaiah 6:1-8

One of the most glorious accounts of angelic activity is found in Isaiah 6. There we discover angels who have six wings and who perpetually cry out "Holy, holy, holy is the LORD of hosts: The whole earth is full of His glory!" Read Revelation 4:1-11 for a similar picture of angels. Angels proclaim the holiness and greatness of God. This is their constant activity. Let us learn from the angels to revere the awesomeness of God.

Family Activity

Tonight you will continue your family movie night by watching the remainder of "It's a Wonderful Life." Remember to note key themes from the movie and especially pay attention to the portrayal of Clarence the angel.

Charles Spurgeon, the Baptist preacher from the 19th century wrote of the holy angels: *It is superstitious to worship angels; it is proper to love them. How free from envy the angels were! How free, too, they were from pride! They were not ashamed to come and tell the news of Christ's birth to humble shepherds. Mark how well they told the story and you will love them.*

Prayer

Our Father in heaven, we thank You for the opportunities that You provide for our family to spend quality time together. Please help our family to grow in our love for You and for one another. Amen.

December 17th

Scripture Reading

Revelation 5

Christmas is a reminder that Jesus Christ is to be central in our lives. Our Scripture reading today makes it very clear that Jesus is to be our focus. He is proclaimed by both the angels and the elders to be "worthy" (9). He is worthy for many reasons including the fact that He is the redeemer who was "slain" (9). Since we have been studying the angels for the past couple of nights make sure that you note from Revelation 5 how the angels respond to Jesus.

Family Activity

Take your notes from the two movie nights and contrast the movie's portrayal of angels with the Bible. What are some of the things that you have learned from the Bible about angels? Find one of the Christmas hymns about angels and compare it to the Bible. Is the hymn based on Scripture, imagination or tradition?

If you are using an Advent Wreath with your family, consider using one of the candles to represent the angels. Generally the 4 smaller candles that surround the larger candle all represent characters from the Christmas story. The large white candle in the middle is a reminder of Jesus and His superiority over everyone and everything else. Praise the Lord for the angels.

Prayer

Our Father in heaven, we confess that there is no one and nothing higher than You. Help us to take the lessons learned today and apply them to our lives. Help us to saturate our hearts and minds with the Bible as we seek to think more correctly about the incarnation of our Lord. Amen.

December 18

Scripture Reading

Luke 1:1-25

A period of about 400 years separates the Old Testament from the New Testament. Though there was no prophetic word during that time that does not mean that God was silent (remember our "4 C's" from a previous study). In Luke chapter one God breaks his prophetic silence and speaks. The message of Christmas is the message of God communicating with His people. Let us hear the word of truth.

Today we focus on the forerunner of Jesus. His name was John. Our verses today tell us of John's pre-birth announcement by the angel to Zechariah. God is wonderfully answering the prayers of Zechariah and of his wife Elizabeth with the promised birth of John (13). Their child would be "great in the sight of the Lord" and be "filled with the Holy Spirit" (15).

John would have a great purpose for his life. He would "...turn many of the children of Israel to the Lord their God" and He would "go before Him in the spirit and power of Elijah to turn the hearts of the fathers to the children and the disobedient to the wisdom of the just, to make ready a people prepared for the Lord" (17).

Family Activity

Elisabeth and Zechariah were too old to have a child. This makes the birth of John even more amazing and demonstrative of the power of God. Compare the announcement about the birth of John with that concerning Jesus (see Luke 1:5-25, 26-38; Matthew 1:18-25). Before the President of the United States visits a town, advance men are sent ahead of his arrival. What is their job? In what ways would John prepare the way for the coming of Jesus Christ? Read Luke 1:57-80 and Mark 1:1-11.

Prayer

Our Father in heaven, thank You for sending a forerunner to prepare the way for Jesus. Help us to be more like John and to be bold spokespersons for the truth. Amen.

December 19th

Scripture Reading

John 1:1

John 1:1 reminds us that Jesus is God! It is essential that you know the truth about Jesus as revealed in the Bible. In order to be forgiven of your sins you must believe in Jesus. You are not allowed to believe in an imaginary Jesus or even the Jesus of popular opinion in order to be saved. You must believe in the true Jesus Christ. If you had been living in the 3rd and 4th century you may have encountered a teacher by the name of Arius. Arius taught that Jesus was indeed a very exalted creature—similar to the Father but a created being nonetheless. His view was different from that of Thomas the apostle who said to Jesus in John 20:28, "My Lord and my God."

There have been a number of errant views concerning Jesus throughout history. In fact it is essential to inquire of any teacher what his or her estimation is of Jesus Christ. If the teaching is wrong about Christ then you must reject it. It is dangerous to embrace errant teaching about Christ and His gospel (see Galatians 1).

The Bible teaches both the full humanity and the full deity of Jesus Christ. Jesus had a human body, He was born, He developed physically, He became tired, and ultimately Jesus died. Jesus rose from the dead in a real body and Jesus ascended to heaven in His resurrected human body. Jesus had a real mind and real emotions and yet Jesus was sinless. Yes, Jesus was fully human but as Thomas proclaimed He was truly God. Have you acknowledged Jesus as your "Lord and God?"

Family Activity

Write down and memorize I John 4:1-3. *Beloved, do not believe every spirit, but test the spirits, whether they are of God; because many false prophets have gone out into the world. By this you know the Spirit of God: Every spirit that confesses that Jesus Christ has come in the flesh is of God, and every spirit that does not confess that Jesus Christ has come in the flesh is not of God. And this is the spirit of Antichrist, which you have heard was coming, and is now already in the world."*

Talk with your children about the importance of believing the truth about Jesus!

Prayer

Our Father thank You for the Bible which informs us of the true nature of Christ. Please help our family to acknowledge and demonstrate that Jesus Christ is Lord. Amen.

December 20th

Scripture Reading

John 14:1-2; Revelation 21

Have you ever been homesick? The Christian should have homesickness for heaven. The Bible teaches that heaven is a real place where real people will spend a real eternity with a real Savior who really came to the cradle in Bethlehem and really lived a righteous life. He really died on the cross as the substitutionary sacrifice for His people, and really ascended to heaven, where today He really sits at the right hand of God praying for His people. One day He will really return. His people will really go to heaven!

What does heaven have to do with Christmas? "So Christ was offered once to bear the sins of many. To those who eagerly wait for Him, He will appear a second time, apart from sin, for salvation" (Hebrews 9:28). Christ came to earth to bear the sins of His people. Bethlehem was his first stop on the way to Calvary. Over the cradle of Bethlehem loomed the shadow of the cross of Calvary. Yet, beyond Calvary was Heaven to which Jesus ascended and from which He will return for His people. Without Bethlehem there is no eternal home for believers. Without heaven, Bethlehem loses its significance.

This Christmas season, as you think about Christ and lead your family to focus on Him, think about heaven. From heaven Jesus came. To heaven He ascended. From heaven He will return. To heaven all of His people will go. As you remember the cradle, think of the cross and don't forget to keep your eyes fixed on heaven.

Family Activity

Ask your children to tell you what they think heaven is really like. Write down their answers. Find some of the key passages in the Bible that refer to heaven and read them out loud. Have your children read along with you. Help your children to develop a biblical under-standing of heaven. On a sheet of paper draw a picture that illustrates how Bethlehem is connected to Calvary, how Calvary is connected to heaven and how all three places are connected to each other.

Prayer

Our Father in heaven, thank You for heaven. Lord I pray that You will take each member of our family to be with You in heaven. Help us to be faithful as a family to learn and embrace the gospel of Jesus Christ. Amen.

December 21st

Scripture Reading

Luke 1:26-27

Who was Mary the mother of Jesus? That question has been asked often. A variety of answers have been given. More girls have been named Mary than perhaps any other name. People are intrigued by this lady of antiquity and some aspire to be more like her. However, there have been many errors about Mary in the history of Christianity. Some have taught her perpetual virginity even after the birth of Christ. Though the Bible is very clear that Mary was a virgin when Jesus was conceived and remained a virgin until his birth, the Bible nowhere indicates that Mary remained a virgin following the birth of Jesus. In fact, the Bible speaks of the brothers and sisters of Jesus (Mark 6:3). During the middle ages it was taught that

Mary herself was conceived without original sin. The doctrine of the Immaculate Conception is the result of such thinking. The Bible nowhere supports that view. In Luke 1 Mary refers to God as her "Savior." That indicates that Mary saw herself as a sinner in need of a Savior. Mary was and is often viewed as one who intercedes as a mediator for Christians and as a sort of co-redeemer with Christ. The Bible never teaches such a thing. The Bible teaches that there is only one mediator and that is Jesus Himself (I Timothy 2:5).

There are shrines to Mary all over the world and countless people pray to Mary and look to her as their heavenly representative. Some people even claim that Mary appears to them and that she is an object of worship.

Biblically speaking Mary was the chosen one of God to be the earthly mother of Jesus Christ. She called herself a "maidservant of the Lord" (Luke 1:38). As the mother of Jesus she was with him throughout His earthly life (John 19:25-27). Mary continued on as a follower of Jesus.

Mary was a woman of moral purity (Luke 1:27) but nevertheless a sinner (Luke 1:47). God's amazing grace was upon her (Luke 1:28, 30, 42, 48). Mary was obedient to the commands of God (Luke 1:38), grounded in Scripture (Luke 1:46-55) and a worshipper God.

Let us be faithful this Christmas to have a biblical regard for Mary. Elizabeth referred to Mary as "Blessed among women" (Luke 1:42) and as "The mother of my Lord" (43). Mary said of herself that "all generations shall call me blessed" (48). We should never have errant views about Mary and we must not worship or pray to her. Nevertheless we should honor her as a blessed mother of the faith. We should worship · God for choosing and demonstrating His grace to Mary and we should imitate her faith.

Family Activity

Already this month you have read Luke 1:46-55. Read it again. This time look specifically for examples of Mary's godly character. Examine closely this text and jot down truths about Mary. Lead your children to understand that we must all learn to humbly yield our lives to God. Read Luke 1:38 again about Mary's response to the message of the angel.

Prayer

Our Father in heaven, thank You for the example of Mary. Forgive us if we have failed to honor her as the mother of our Lord and a mother of the faith. Help us to rightly regard her and not to fall into the errors of exalting her to a place of worship. Help us to imitate her faithfulness. Thank You for choosing Mary and in choosing her, demonstrating Your amazing grace! Amen.

December 22nd

Scripture Reading

Responsive Reading from *Hebrews 1*

Parent: *"But when He again brings the firstborn into the world, He says:"*
Family: *"Let all the angels of God worship Him."*
Parent: *"But to the Son He says…"*
Family: *"Your throne, O God, is forever and ever; A scepter of righteousness is the scepter of your kingdom. You have loved righteousness and hated lawlessness; Therefore God, Your God, has anointed You with the oil of gladness more than your companions."*
Parent: *"And: You, LORD, in the beginning laid the foundations of the earth"*
Family: *"And the heavens are the work of your hands. They will perish, but You remain."*

God commands that the angels worship Jesus. The Scripture reading today is a reminder that Jesus is God, He has an eternal throne, He is righteous and He is the Creator. Have each member of your family praise Jesus for these great truths about Him.

Family Activity

Sing a Christmas hymn.

Ask: How can our family celebrate Christmas in a way that honors God? What are your ideas? What are some of the opportunities that we have to glorify God this Christmas season?

Prayer

Our Father in heaven You alone are God. You are eternal. Your Son is eternal. Help us to discover ways to glorify You during the Christmas season. Amen.

December 23rd

Scripture Reading

Deuteronomy 11:19

There are many words that are spoken this time of year about Christmas. Christians have the responsibility and the opportunity to teach "God's words." God has given us a great classroom—the universe. All of creation offers us the opportunity to see the glory of God. That being true we must focus our attention especially on the words of the Bible and teach them to our children all the time. This is done in the regular activities of the day. We are to impress the character of God on the hearts of our children by helping them see the world through the lens of Scripture. This is a Christian worldview—a godly way of looking at the world. As you look at the world this Christmas season, what do you see? You certainly see competing worldviews. There are those who would have any reference to Christ removed from Christmas, simply referring to this season as the Winter Holidays. However, the Christian is concerned that Christ would be seen as great at Christmas and all of the time. Christ is to be always at the forefront of our thinking, whether we work or play. If we have to push thoughts of Christ out of our mind to engage in a particular activity, then we have put ourselves in a position where we cannot bring positive glory to God. We are to eat, drink, wash dishes, sing, and celebrate Christmas to the glory of God. Life is for His glory.

Family Activity

Go Christmas caroling with your family (you might also include your church and other friends) in the neighborhood tonight. Devise a song sheet with the words of Christmas songs to take with you. Stuff some envelopes to give to your neighbors with information about your church, a Christmas message, and an invitation to your house for snacks following the time of caroling.

When your neighbors arrive at your home, share a brief testimony about the true meaning of Christmas and enjoy a time of dessert.

Prayer

Our Father in heaven, thank You for our neighbors. Help our family to be a good witness to our neighbors during the Christmas season and always. Amen.

December 24th

Scripture Reading

Luke 2:1-20

One of the highlights of our Christmas season when I was a child was the Christmas Eve reading of Luke chapter two. Christmas Eve was a time to open a present (usually new pajamas), eat our Christmas Eve meal (usually oyster stew) and have some cake. However, the highlight came when my dad would read from Luke chapter two. This is a tradition that I have continued with my wife and five daughters. This passage is most recognizable as "The Christmas Story." Consider making this a part of your Christmas Eve activities.

Family Activity

If you are using an Advent Wreath, you will light the fourth candle on your wreath. Light the candle after reading Luke chapter two. You will light all of the candles except the middle candle tonight. This is in anticipation of Christmas morning when your Advent Wreath will be aglow with the four surrounding candles lit and the Christ candle shining brightly.

Many churches have a Christmas Eve candlelight service. The candlelight service has become a treasured tradition in our church. If your church has Christmas Eve services then go and worship with your fellow believers.

Do you already have a Christmas Eve dinner that is traditional at your home? If not consider a stew or chili or some other meal that will become the standard meal on this extraordinary night.

Don't forget to sing some Christmas carols before going to bed.

Third Lord's Day

Scripture Reading

Colossians 1:13-18

Everything was created by Christ and for Christ. That is the message of the Bible. Our Scripture reading today communicates those truths and also the fact that Jesus is the "head of the body, the church..." What a great passage for reading and meditation on the Lord's Day. Today you will gather with your church family and be reminded in doing so that you were created by and for Christ and that He is the head of His church. Church is not an insignificant option for the Christian; rather, it is a joyful community of those who have been saved by grace for the glory of Jesus Christ. Jesus is the life of the church. The Christmas season can be a powerful reminder of the glory of Jesus.

Family Activity

Tonight you will light the third Advent candle as a part of your family activities. You can choose for the candles to represent any of the characters in the Christmas Story. Perhaps tonight you will choose to let the candle represent the angels. Make it a point each Lord's Day to pray for your pastor and church.

Prayer

Our Father, thank you that You love and are the head of Your church. Please help our family to treasure Your people and joyfully gather with them for congregational worship. Amen.

Fourth Lord's Day

Scripture Reading

I Timothy 3:15-17

The church belongs to God! Embracing
that statement will help you to better
understand and appreciate life in the body
of Christ. It will also help to keep you from
seeking to infringe upon that which
belongs to Another by importing your own
opinions and ideas about the church.
Chapter 21 paragraph 1 in the Westminster
Confession reads:

*The light of nature showeth that there is a God,
who hath lordship and sovereignty over all, is
good, and doth good unto all, and is therefore to
be feared, loved, praised, called upon, trusted in,
and served, with all the heart, and with all the
soul, and with all the might. But the acceptable
way of worshiping the true God is instituted by*

himself, and so limited by his own revealed will, that he may not be worshiped according to the imaginations and devices of men, or the suggestions of Satan, under any visible representation, or any other way not prescribed in the Holy Scripture.

This is sometimes called the Regulative Principle of worship meaning that God has ordained through His Word *how* He is to be worshipped in His church. There are a variety of perceptions concerning the Regulative Principle. One way that it might be stated is that the church must do what the New Testament commands her to do when she gathers for worship. She must not do what the Scripture does not command. She is free to do that which is consistent with the Bible. On this last point, for example, there are those who think that because the New Testament is silent on the church using musical instruments, the church should not therefore use them in worship. However, if one holds to the view that the Regulative Principle of worship permits the Christian to do that which is consistent with the whole of Scripture, then one would be free to use musical instruments in the public worship of the church. The main point is that God is not silent about worship. His Word is to inform and direct His people in congregational worship.

Our Scripture reading today reminds us not only that Christ owns the church but that the church is the "pillar and ground of the truth" (15). The truth that is to be held up is summarized in Vs. 16 *God was manifested in the flesh, justified in the Spirit, seen by angels, preached among the Gentiles, believed on in the world, received up in glory.*

That passage of Scripture summarizes the message of Christmas. The Lord's Day is a reminder, as we gather with the people of God, that we belong to God and we exist to stand on and hold up the truth about Jesus.

Family Activity

Have a family question and answer session tonight. Ask questions such as "What is the church?" "Who does the church belong to?" "What is the purpose of the church?"

Prayer

Our Father, thank You for establishing the church, giving her the truth to stand on and to hold up. Help our church to be faithful to allow only Your Word to regulate the worship of the church to Your glory. Thank You for the reminder that Christ is to be central in Your church. Amen.

A Catechism for Christmas

Christians have been using catechisms since the early days of the New Testament church. A catechism is simply a means of instruction using questions and answers. The catechism leader asks a question and listens for a correct response. Christians from a variety of denominational and independent traditions have used catechisms.

Catechisms have primarily been used as a means of instructing children of all ages. However, adults have benefited as well from such systematic instruction about the great doctrines of the Bible. Catechisms can also be written to teach specific passages of Scripture to our children. The catechism below can be used to help you teach part of Luke chapter 2 to your children this Christmas season. Why not consider using good, theologically sound catechisms to instruct your children? If your children are not yet Christians, think of the foundation of truth that will be theirs if the Lord chooses to open their hearts to the gospel.

Catechism from Luke 2:8-14

Q. Who was living out in the fields the night that Jesus was born?

A. *"Now there were in the same country shepherds living out in the fields, keeping watch over their flock by night"* (8).

Q. Who stood in the presence of the shepherds and how did the shepherds respond?

A. *"And behold, an angel of the Lord stood before them, and the glory of the Lord shone around them, and they were greatly afraid"*(9)

Q. What did the angel say?

A. *"Then the angel said to them, 'Do not be afraid, for behold, I bring you good tidings of great joy which shall be to all people. For there is born to you this day in the city of David a Savior who is Christ the Lord. And this will be the sign to you. You will find a Babe wrapped in swaddling cloths, lying in a manger"* (10-12).

Q. Who appeared with the angel and what did they say?

A. *"And suddenly there was with the angel a multitude of the heavenly host praising God and saying: 'Glory to God in the highest, And on earth peace, goodwill toward men'"* (13-14).

Family Activity

Now, you give it a try. Take the remainder of the verses from Luke 2:1-20 and develop your own catechism. Use it with your children and by the end of the Christmas season it is likely that you and your entire family will have memorized these 20 verses. Consider using the Westminster Shorter Catechism, The Heidelberg Catechism or The Baptist Catechism as a part of your family worship activities for the New Year.

Conclusion

The evening in late October was filled with laughter and awe. Laughter at the expressions and comments of each family member, awe at the providence of God.

We rounded the corner on our "night walk" and heard the music of the Salem Band with the wind of life filling their instruments. The children were delighted when, spontaneously, the quiet autumn evening was suddenly filled with music. We listened with smiles as we stood on the street corner surrounded by a community that first came to life in the mid-1700's. For a moment we were back in time listening, watching and feeling communion with the past that was engaging our present.

We were all surprised to find the side door unlocked. Slowly we opened it, carefully glancing inside. Before we knew it we had entered the building and were slowly winding our way up the stairs. At the top, that which had first fancied our ears and captured our imagination on the street corner below, now engaged our eyes as we could see the room from which the music originated. They practiced and practiced and practiced again.

When the announcement came that in only two weeks, rehearsal would begin for the Christmas concert, the aroma of the holidays permeated the building, flowed through an open window and into the night air that soon would touch our faces and fill our hearts with joy.

As we walked away and back into the night, I realized something unexpected had occurred. It was one of those moments that time cannot erase for it is etched indelibly upon the heart. God had surprised us with music. He had allowed me to hear again from the voices of my girls the love of the heart. We laughed and picked up the pace for the girls had a story to tell Mommy about the music in the night.

Family worship at Christmas time is like that music. By God's grace the aroma of worshipping God as a family can waft through the generations and impact great-grand children with the beauty and glory of God and the sweetness of a God-centered family.

The Christmas season is a big deal in the Rhodes' household. It starts around Thanksgiving and ends on New Years Day. In between we have a number of "essential" activities. If you come to our home during the holidays, you may be offered something sweet to eat that either my wife or our children have cooked. If you stay for dinner, we will pull enough chairs to the table so that we can sit and talk a while.

Whether it is around the table or somewhere else in your home, make sure that you spend regular time with your family in worship of God. This Christmas is a good time to get started.

About the Author

Ray Rhodes, Jr. is President of Nourished in the Word Ministries. Nourished in the Word is a teaching, writing, and church planting ministry. Ray and Lori have been married for 20 years and are blessed with five daughters: Rachel, Hannah, Sarah, Mary and Lydia. To schedule Ray to speak for your next conference, please contact him at **www.nourishedintheword.org.** Lori is also available to speak to ladies groups on a variety of issues related to godly womanhood. Visit Lori on the Web at **www.nitw4ladies.blogspot.com**

Ray and his family live in North Georgia.

Other Related Titles from Solid Ground

Solid Ground Christian Books is delighted to offer several books from Thomas H. Gallaudet and his friend Horace Hooker. The following books are in print and ready to ship.

THE CHILD'S BOOK ON THE SOUL by Thomas H. Gallaudet is the most remarkable of all the books written by the man known as *The Father of Education to the Deaf in America*. This book addresses the reality of the never-dying soul in words that can be understood by a five year old. It is this book that was used more than any of his others to bring children all over the world to seek the living God.

THE CHILD'S BOOK ON THE FALL by Thomas H. Gallaudet is the sequel to *The Child's Book on the Soul*. It is an outstanding little book that introduces the significance of Genesis 3 at a level that can be understood by a child. This is a powerful book that will magnify the seriousness of sin and the glory of God's grace in the Gospel.

THE CHILD'S BOOK ON REPENTANCE by T.H. Gallaudet is a book that examines the specific area of repentance through the medium of dialogues between a mother and her three children. Once again this is a book that examines a critic issue in a way that can be understood by children. The author does an especially thorough job of exposing the danger of incomplete and false repentance.

THE CHILD'S BOOK ON THE SABBATH by Horace Hooker was one of Gallaudet's closest friends. He here lends his efforts to address an important matter in a most gracious and balanced way. Like his friend, Hooker uses the dialogues between a mother and her three children to address the various doctrinal and practical issues that surround the issue of the Christian view of the Sabbath.

THE YOUTH'S BOOK OF NATURAL THEOLOGY by Thomas Gallaudet is a book for children a bit older than the previous four titles we have published. In this volume the author again uses a series of dialogues and helpful pictures to lead the child to understand everything that can be learned about God from the world around us.

Call us Toll Free at **1-866-789-7423**
Send us an e-mail at **sgcb@charter.net**
Visit our web site at **www.solid-ground-books.com**

Other Solid Ground Titles

In addition to the volume which you hold in your hand, Solid Ground is honored to offer many other uncovered treasure, many for the first time in more than a century:

Another Christmas Title from Solid Ground

In addition to *Family Worship for the Christmas Season* we are delighted to offer the following title especially written for young children by a beloved servant of Christ:

The Truth About Christmas
By Peter Jeffery

Peter Jeffery, a retired pastor from Wales, is not only a gifted preacher and writer, he is also a father and grandfather. In these stories about Christmas he combines his gift of teaching with his love for children. These stories will speak to the hearts of children and those who love them.

In the author's own words:

"Many of these stories came out of my experiences with my own children and grandchildren. Christmas is an exciting time for youngsters but they need to know the truth about this amazing story of God's love and grace. The truth about Christmas will not destroy the excitement, rather it will give it meaning and reason."

Printed in the United States
200332BV00002B/388-645/A